PLACES IN POETRY

poetry Pt today

PLACES IN POETRY

Edited by Rebecca Mee

First published in Great Britain in 1999 by Poetry
Today, an imprint of
Penhaligon Page Ltd, Remus House, Coltsfoot Drive,
Woodston, Peterborough. PE2 9JX

A Catalogue record for this book is available from the
British Library

ISBN 1 862 26568 2

Typesetting and layout, Penhaligon Page Ltd, England.
Printed and bound by Forward Press Ltd, England

Foreword

Places in Poetry is a compilation of poetry, featuring some of our finest poets. This book gives an insight into the essence of modern living and deals with the reality of life today. We think we have created an anthology with a universal appeal.

There are many technical aspects to the writing of poetry and *Places in Poetry* contains free verse and examples of more structured work from a wealth of talented poets.

Poetry is a coat of many colours. Today's poets write in a limitless array of styles: traditional rhyming poetry is as alive and kicking today as modern free verse. Language ranges from easily accessible to intricate and elusive.

Poems have a lot to offer in our fast-paced 'instant' world. Reading poems gives us an opportunity to sit back and explore ourselves and the world around us.

Contents

If He'd Let Me

There is a man sweet and kind
Whose face is a gem
When he looks at mine.
I see him always walking by
And yet I'll love him till I die.
His body, movement and his smile,
His wit, his voice, makes my heart excite
And I know not why.
But if he'd let me
I'd love him till I die.
Cupid is winged
Please look at me,
Let his love come to me.
Change the earth
Or change this key
But if he'd let me
I'd love him
Till the day I die.

Elainea

A Journey From Madrid To Valencia

I saw the sun on the fields of toil
It glistened on the water
And blew the verdant paddies
As a fitful tide.

Flat bottomed boats on a mirrored sea,
Sombrero straws coolie-like
And a bamboo cane.
A vista on a Chinese screen.

Angela Cheyne

Hell To Heaven

Hell to heaven and back again,
That's what this place's about.
Never looking over your shoulder,
Frightened, to go on out.
Sure! Crime is on the increase
That there is no doubt,
But it's in such a small proportion
'Tis hardly any amount.

Les J Croft

Kassala ~ The Hadendawa Women

The Hadendawa women, dried blossoms in the acacia shade
Their tobes' acid colours burn, stifle.
Rings through their noses, terror in their eyes.

Sometimes they litter the ground in front of the clinic.
Sometimes the police move them on.

They resist; it is *their* place,
Their time for hope among the hopeless years;
Pills, injections, substitutes for kindliness.

Around them Sudanese, Kassala people,
In tobe, jelabya or western dress,
Walk, cycle, greet and talk
With all the ease of sun-people.

Why then do these women,
Immaculate conceptions of sun and sand
Shrink from the pain of breathing
The same air?

Caustic islands flowering harsh anxiety,
Ripped from deep desert,
Now rooted,
Shallow, crippled, hungry-rooted
In this town.

Duncan Logan

4

New Zealand

Clean, crisp and cold is the New Zealand air
Mountains with snow on everywhere
The occasional town nestled deep in the base
For a country so small, there is so much space

Lakes and rivers, crystal clear
Provide a central point for people here
Activities of speed, danger and height
Keep people enthralled from day through to night

Miles of mountain roads with no-one around
The occasional bird is the only sound
Sheep grazing on endless fields of grass
Oblivious to the occasional cars that pass

Bright, sunny mornings and cold frosty nights
T-shirts are replaced by jackets zipped tight
Early to bed and early to rise
Wandering freely without any ties

Everywhere that you look is a postcard scene
Mountains majestic, rivers serene
Beauty surrounds you wherever you go
A country so healthy you leave with a glow

Paula Boston

Not Constantinople

Minarets inspirally
The baths a waltz with agony
On weary feet and thirsting deep
Through markets wild and labyrinthed streets
Across Bosphorous wide to Asia fair
A snapshot view of beauty deep
Long will the hubbub stay with me
In Istanbul, I dared to dream

Dave Downes

Land Of My Fathers

A land of rugged mountains, valleys lush and deep
Images within my mind I shall forever keep
A land that's laced with culture, a pride that never fails
Wherever I shall wander, my thoughts return to Wales
Of steep mountain slopes with white dots of sheep
A trusty old shepherd his vigil to keep
His eyes ever watchful from evening to dawn
At this miracle time when new lambs will be born
Making it's journey through cool pastures green
The tinkling sound of a rolling stream
Wending and winding lazy and slow
It's journey to end in the sea far below
In the heart of the valley where ploughmen till
An old farmhouse rests at the foot of a hill
The farmer's wife is sitting there
At close of day in her rocking-chair
Her daily tasks over, with time to bide
In peaceful content at her own fireside
The old village church, a warm evening in Spring
Where friendly folk gather and rafters will ring
Home of the choir, the poet, the bard
Great men of rugby, a pack tough and hard
A grandmother's home where the family gathers
Traditions are strong in this Land of My Fathers'
My heart sing with joy, a sight to behold
Where the hills meet the sea through a carpet of gold
In search of a meal, the gulls' hungry cry
Resound through the bay as they circle the sky
A portrait of beauty, the mountains, the vales
God's special creation, My Country - My Wales.

Barbara Davies

7

Camden Market

From the darkness of the tube,
we step out into the unknown
The masses are everywhere,
making the pavement invisible
We're confronted by the soldiers of the left,
claiming revolution is nigh
We turn right and head for the Lock,
noises and smells attacking or senses,
The mad, the beautiful and the way out,
lighten up the overcast day
In and out of the stalls we romp,
searching for bargains and a chance to haggle
Slowly but surely we give in to temptation,
as we greedily devour fresh doughnuts
We trek up and down North London's golden mile,
fascinated by the bizarre and the tacky
Finally we beat a retreat,
to a favoured watering hole
Sitting together exhausted but happy,
observing the madness of our market

Alex Alexandrou

Across The Bay

The sun is shining across the bay
The view is clear and bright,
The honey coloured buildings stand
Shining in the crystal light.

But when the day is dull and wet
The lines are soft and blurred,
And through the curtain of the rain
We glimpse another world.

A world of knights and Saracens
In coats of mail ashine.
Their lances glinting in the sun
And pennants stream on high.

Their horses all caparisoned
In red and blue and tasselled gold,
Stamping, snorting into battle
Carrying the Knights so bold.

You hear the clash of mace and lance
As the battle rages on,
The heavy thud of iron shod hooves
Charging through the fighting throng.

As the rain begins to clear
The sun dispels the magic scene,
All is now hard edged and modern
No more we see what might have been.

The terraced land is green and peaceful
No more sounds of clashing steel,
Where Infidels and Christians battled
Men now cultivate the fields.

Long ago the Knights of Malta
Fought the Infidel and won,
Now the island lies serene
Beneath the Mediterranean sun.

Edna Cosby

Empire Of The Dead

As I crossed the threshold
Into the Empire of the dead
The breath of the city
Passed its last exhalation
As I crept through
The ornamented graffitied ruins
Of it's society
Antiquity's artists
Paint the vandalised decimated
Lime beds of stone death
With portrayals of their own demise
Into obsoleteness
The eerieness of this soundless place
Was brutally ended
When the deluge fell
From a sepulchral heaven
Offspring of the trees
Strewn the complex paths
In the cobblestone maze

Massacred
By silent bullets of December rain
In the distance
War cries of reclamation
Accompany the symphonies of war
Fighting the tyrant
Seeking liberation
From his sixth circle incarceration
An explosion underground
Damages the revolution's faction
Cause for peace

Four followers of innocence killed
One had no face
For which to scream
Two had limbs torn by shrapnel
Unable to reach help
The final was slain in half
By glass and infused steel

Tears of the guardians
Soaked the night
In cold guilt
At the failure to protect

Consummations forever
Bare the scars
Plagued and faded
Strays from the city
Awaken and leave to hunt
Whilst others scour devoid graves
I found one sleeping in the gouged
Stomach
Of a dead rock singer
Killed by fame and muse

As I paused for rest
At the top of the pyre
The musted air or rigor mortis
Had me in its stranglehold
A resurrected feline chimera
Perches itself beside me
Its black velveteen's entwines
In a caress of relapse
With the excrescence's
That mottle its grey flesh

Hypnotised in its song
The chimera
Tells me of failures old
Those yet to come
Watching the city scorched
Contemplating my next duel
With yet another nemesis.

Rob Gregg

Northern Hell

Soldiers, soldiers,
Across the barricade.
Fighting, fighting,
Bombs, guns, grenades.
The children play,
Such a grim day.
Catholics, 'Prods',
Whose war?
Not God's.
Who wins?
Who sins?
Northern hell.
Bloody hell.

M B Chissim

Dawn - Bodmin Moor, Cornwall

We crossed the Moor in crystal light, before the heat of day,
And watched Red Kites and Sparrow Hawks, glide in search of prey.
The distant Tors so pearly white, as islands in a sea,
Shimmered in the silver mist, that floated soft and free.

Today the sky, no lemon peach, the sun, no yellow gold,
A luminescent dazzling white, that let the Moor unfold.
We held our breath, just you and I, and saw this magic scene.
We closed our eyes and felt the touch of Heaven pure and clean.

The seconds passed, we felt the warmth, of early morning sun,
And saw the floating shrouds of mist, disperse and melt in fun.
Such memories of special times, of places far and near,
Stay only days, but one like this, will never disappear.

Another journey, apart this time, just you or I alone,
We'll see a day of pure white light, a dawn to be our own.
But I'll remember, and so will you, that journey 'cross the Moor,
The Crystal light and silver mist, we spied through Heavens' door.

Janet Allen

Isle Of Skye

From mainland shore to island shore
Across the deep, the ferries ply.
The symmetry of mountain range
Draws close the Isle of mystic Skye.

In number few, small hamlets quietly bide,
Whereas Portree, is a bustling town indeed.
Welcome seats furnish its quaint and charming square,
Winding steps and alleys to the pretty harbour lead.

Wild purple heather carpets the stark moors;
Mysterious lochs reflect the Cuillins sombre heights.
Roads weave in loneliness, and buzzards seek their prey,
Hovering, they silently keep their quarry in their sights.

Oft in early day a shrouding mist descends,
Beneath the lofty peaks, trapped cloud, whitely lies.
Bleak ruined castles, the scarlet of the rowan,
Such richly passing scenes are balm to weary eyes.

Lizbeth Cooke

To Bath - Revisited

Long ago the Romans built their baths here,
Setting them around a warm bubbling spring,
Centuries on, folk came from far and near
To take the waters, the fashionable thing!
So elegant Bath became in those days,
The Crescent boasted town houses so fine,
Heroines of Jane Austen made their way
Here, the water considered healing wine.
Today the water looks thick and impure,
Crowds marvel at the ancient Roman baths,
See a beauty in the architecture,
A quaintness in the pedestrian paths.
From a hot spring bubbling up from the ground,
Sprang a city where elegance abounds.

Pat Heppel

Green And Pleasant Land

Green is a lovely colour. Fairies dressed
(They say!) in green when they would look their best.
Cool curling waves of summer seas are green,
That slide with gracious swell the rocks between.

Green lawns for weary feet are welcoming,
Green fires are lit on larch and beech in spring.
Green fields, green woods, green parklands speak of rest,
Green hedge gives shelter to the blackbird's nest.

Green gleam the eyes of little friendly beast,
Green hang the swelling fruits for promised feast.
Green grows the western sky when sun is down,
And England's robed in green from hem to crown.

Kathleen M Hatton

Around The World In Poetry (Or In 30 Days)

I travel over land and sea
I travel each day - travel in my mind

Then one day I pack my bags
On impulse I climb onto my bike.
It's John O'Groats to Land's End or bust.

I board the train in Doncaster
I travel down to Bude
I cycle on to the End of Land
Land's End my destination.

I climb my bike and cycle on,
Thirty miles a day.
I stop for coffee, stop for lunch, for
Supper and for drinks.
Each night I find a jolly dig and
Sleep beneath the moon.

The days are long
The nights are short.
Two punctures, two flat tyres.
A migraine held me up one day
And then I soldier on.

The days are warm
I ring them home
They think that I've gone mad.
Is my money going to last?
Around my world with me

I travel into Scotland
Many miles to go.
But I will reach my John O'Groats
My bicycle and me.

Janet Cavill

18

City Lights

I hear the sounds
of jazz on abandoned
city neon streets,
staggering whores and pimp boys
playing lost lovers' games
on swirling week old yellowed newspapers,
the drunk forgot to
take home his blanket
and the night wind howls
pagan rhythms
in boogie-woogie souls,
haunting images of
a time when I was yet unborn
inside the bodies of junkie poets
and glamorously dressed men
in women's clothing,
parading half naked,
the nun turned her head and walks on
down grimy late night streets,
the feral child
wild eyed in confusion
stops
for just one moment
to hear the crashing
of broken glass
the crashing
   of broken lives
   broken promises
   broken memories
of primordial ecstasy
in half shadows
back alleys
rusted fire escapes
I hear the jazz
from rooftops,
              city streets.

Roberta James-Harrison

The Sphinx Of Egypt

Under the sun 'neath the shade of the Sphinx
    Where Cairo and the desert part
There lived a dark eyed Arab girl
    who died of a broken heart

She lived in a city of white and gold
    Palm trees and ever blue sky
But no one in Egypt knew the truth
    not even the Sphinx on high

She sold her perfume in the bazaar
    where travellers meet in a while
And many a man bought scent from her
    for the sake of that Arab girl's smile

But one stayed longer than the rest
    he came from a far off land
And that little Arab girl danced with joy
    when he bent and kissed her hand

She gave her love to this foreigner
    who swore by his God above
That he would be her guiding star
    and nothing would kill his love

But little she knew of the Western race
    and the price she'd have to pay
Till a boat went sailing down the Canal
    sailing further and further away

Slowly she walked from that old bazaar
    through Cairo's winding streets
Ashamed, disgraced, a fallen soul
    afraid of her race to meet

Out in the desert of silence
    in the desert she seeks her rest
Not a cry was heard from that Arab girl
    nor the baby that clings to her breast.

Lachlan Taylor

20

Hawaii

Saurian peaks pierce azure sky.
Crystal streams cascade through ravines.
Jewelled wings over exotic blooms,
Poinsettias line the highway.

Jagged rocks on black sugar sand
strewn by an unseen giant hand.
Refuge against their monarch's wrath -
Pu 'uhonua o Honaunnau!

Ocean rushes through Blow Hole.
Water jet showers passers-by.
Rainbow droplets fall in a curtain
hiding *Hanuauma* Bay

Pele's blood pours hotly from her side
in molten crimson gore;
building more land for her people
to dwell on evermore.

Fuchsia Coles

North African Camp: Tunisia 1943

To what dark centre of the East
Have the banished rivers gone?
In what strange valley do they feast -
Gods whose beauty flamed and shone
On dancing waters in the dawn?
Are the vanished rivers dead
Or do they flow by greener lawn
Where imperial rulers tread
In clear and gentle English light?
Now these firs and slender pines,
Trees whose graceful shaded sight
Here by England's tented lines
Mocks the mirages of death
While the west winds' whispered breath
Trembling in the desert air
Cools the fevers of my brain.
O what sweet branches and how fair
Can live on the edge of the desert plain.

Uvedale Tristram

Kent On A Summer's Day

Kent, England's garden of wealth and of riches,
filled with the beauty and glory of God;
meadows and rivulets, hedgerows and ditches
and here and there paths where the pilgrims have trod.

Farmhouses deep in the valleys lie sleeping;
sunlight shines down on the soft waving corn.
men in their shirtsleeves are toiling and reaping,
working all day from the first break of dawn.

Fruit in the orchards is ripening and growing;
masses of flowers are found everywhere.
Softly the breezes sigh; rivers are flowing
down to the sea in the fresh morning air.

Up in the heavens a brown lark is singing,
trilling it high notes as, soaring above,
high in the sunshine, its tender voice ringing,
out of its heart pours the sweetness of love.

And I as I lie in the sun, lone and dreary
and see spread before me such beauty as this,
no longer can I feel so sad and so weary
but filled with contentment, with peace and with bliss.

Muriel Woolven

Derbyshire: England

Standing high upon a hill one glorious summer day
I viewed this wonderful land of ours, its beauty before me lay
The greens of lovely England, with its shades of emerald hues
With splashes of the wild flowers, pinks and reds and blues
Grey stone wall dividing fields, like a pattern found
A beautiful woven patchwork, spreading its glory around
Trees like graceful fingers with its hands so gently spread
Covered in fragrant blossoms from its branches softly led
Each path between its beauty wove a wonderment of joy
Rolling slowly through nature's garden, its magic to behold
Each corner turned brings new delights, new pleasures for my eyes
The majestic beauty, crags and fells breathtakingly before me lies
Twisting roads winding high, disappearing from my view
Merge with clouds of fluffy white and skies of brilliant blue
I dearly love this land of mine, this country of my birth
Its beauty if unequalled by any place on earth

Violet Ashton Reid

Cuzco

In a jar . . .
on a shelf,
at a Peruvian museum.
Swayed gently:
an eight month foetus.

Suspended,

forever swimming
I placed a little flower:
a silent prayer.
And the curator muttered,
'Loco gringo.'

Jackie Callow

A Letter From America To Sweden

Dear Mum! You say that Spring has come again
To your fair land.
I long to be there when the lilac blooms.
You understand!
And see the hosts of white anemones
In woodland shade,
To see the trees all decked in tender leaves,
A green parade.
And does the blackbird sing his lullaby,
As evening comes, my heart to pacify?

And Mum, I long to breathe the Summer air
Close by the sea,
And feel the wind of heaven caress my face
Over the lea,
To hear the sound of gentle lapping waves
On sun kissed sand
And feel the tang of salt spray on my lips
In that North land,
See the white seagulls, hear their taunting cry,
And watch the sun go down in crimson sky.

I long to be there when the Summer leaves
Turn gold and red,
To sense the sadness of the passing year
Sweet Summer fled.
I long to roam in sparkling Autumn days
And see the mist,
To be at one with nature as she rests
Her yearly tryst
To know the calm of golden tranquil days,
And in the stillness time to breathe my praise.

And as the shades of Autumn die away
The North winds blow,
Then all the fields put on their Winter gowns
Snow upon snow.
And I hold in my heart the silent woods
In Winter bleak.
Mum, will the bright eyed Robin come again,
His crumbs to seek?
And when I reach the Winter of my days
In my mind's eye I will recall and praise!

Dear daughter mine! This hunger in your heart
This longing deep
And this sweet sense you know not whence it comes
In your soul keep.
It is your Life's heart throbbing for your God,
Till Him you see.
This wondrous world of colour, sight and sound
Helps you to be
Near Him who breathes in all created things
Your restless soul finds peace His nearness brings.

But when your pilgrimage on earth is passed,
Your eyes grow dim,
And all the love and beauty that earth gave
Fulfilled in Him,
For all you gave of love to other lives
Bears fruit one day,
With soul at peace, His radiant face to see,
Your burdens lay.
And know, at last, your longing past recall,
Now met in Him the choicest Rose of all!

Patricia Sköld

The Feast

A Hartebeest was having a feast in the middle of the Masai Mara.
The sun was so hot and the air so dry you would think your were in
the Sahara!

Some Wildebeest came straggling by on their nomadic way
And stopped to chew the cud with him and pass the time of day.

'You're welcome to the grass you see. Take all that you can eat.'
A Lion in his thicket thought, 'I'd much prefer some meat.'

Six Elephants were next to pass and gaily swing along,
Singing and trumpeting a cheery elephant song.

'We'll partake in the feast dear Hartebeest. Our appetites are hearty.
It really is so kind of you to let us join the party.'

Across the plain the lion dozed - his nose between his paws.
He dreamt of meat and chasing game, and woke the Baboon with his
snores.

The Baboon and his tribe hurried down to the feast
And sat for a while with the Hartebeest.

There's Lion up there,' he pointed out.
'He'll not be there long, I very much doubt.'

The Hartebeest replied with ease
'I'll leave exactly when I please.'

A troupe of Monkeys swung through the trees
Chattering away like the whispering breeze.

'Lion's awake. We can see from here.'
'Oh go away, Monkeys. There's nothing to fear.'

A group of Zebras cantered in creating some dust and an awful din.
'Can we join your feast, dear Hartebeest? We'll only take the very
least.'

'Take what you will. Eat to your fill.'
   The Lion made ready for the kill.

The Hartebeest chewed long and hard
But really was never completely on guard.

And the Lion kept low, through the short grass he crept,
Nearer and nearer.
　　　　He was very adept
　　　　　　at this stalking game,
　　　　　　　　as closer and closer to Harte he came.

Then the Lion sprang out at the poor Hartebeest.
With a swipe of a paw and a crunch from his teeth
He pulled down his prey,
And dead on the ground poor Hartebeest lay.

Out where the sun will scorch and burn
there is one lesson all beasts must learn.
They must be alert and always take care.
Of their enemies they must be well aware.

The Hartebeest can live in peace
With Zebra, Monkey and Wildebeest.

But the Lion is swift, and the Cheetah is too
And those who escape are much too few.

Poor Hartebeest is now deceased.

The Lion had him for his feast!

Jackie Stubington

Desert Delights

The sands of time keep shifting
As gently winds do blow
Coming from the north or south
Some where no man goes
Some places are even far too hot
And nothing can survive
Just emptiness and litter void
No will to stay alive
But with wind and with the moisture
God can create a desert rose
But not is some parts of the desert mind
Where nothing ever grows
Some parts can even have cacti
With flowers all in bloom
Gathering moisture from the evening chill
And the stillness of the moon
The desert must have seen lots of moons
What stories it could tell
But then when you stop to think about that
Perhaps it is just as well
For there would be more prodding
More damage even more
With man never stopping to ever say
It's now time to check our score.

A E Jones

The Essence of Scotland

Dark and forbidding is the water deep
Where snow trickles down from the hillside steep,
And swirling mists cast an eerie shroud
As the mountain peak wears a mantle of cloud.
At the foot of the hills in the shade of the rock
Lies an inland lake, a Scottish loch.
Wild and exciting the mountains and glens
What'er lies before, where the river bends.
Waterfalls crash over rocky ravine
Roadside azaleas are burnt tangerine,
The wind whistles loudly - a sad lament
Thro' gnarled old trees that are blackened and bent,
Howling its way with a powerful force
O'er hillsides and waysides chequered with gorse.
As red deer in forests roam wild and free
The essence of Scotland - haunts my memory.

Jean Mackenzie

Around The World In Poetry

There's lots of countries in the world, in a lifetime you won't see them
all
I've been to a few from Paris, to the mountains way up in Napal.
I've been on a camel through Egypt, said prayers in Greece at a
shrine,
Seen temples and Buddha's, done cruises, and drank the best German
wine.
I've seen the black mountains in Austria, the snow on the piste, what
a sight
I've even been in the Canarys while a volcano spit sparks out at night.
I've been to all the Greek islands, swam in lagoons clear and blue,
Travelled around Malta and Rio, I've been to Russia too.
I've savoured the wilds in Malaysia, been to Penang and Frisco Bay,
Kuala Lumpa and Thailand and Bali, I took a donkey through Spain
for a day.
I've rode in a rickshaw, a faluka, in Canada I tried a canoe,
I've been to New York and Ohio, there was always plenty to do.
I've driven a car from Detroit to Kentucky and watched the Country
Queen,
I've seen Portugal and France and Hungary, there's lots of places I've
been.
I've been to Germany and Italy, I've been to Rome once or twice,
Florence was neat, the nude fountains were sweet,
And the cathedral was really quite nice.
The UK has lots of nice places, there's castle in meadows so green
There's rivers and valleys and mountains and lots of things I've not
seen,
I've travelled with friends and family, I've even travelled alone,
The world has so much to offer, but it's always so nice to come home.

C Freeman

To Cyprus

O' Isle of love and mystery
How can they know your strife?
Those who come for sea and sun,
Escaping from their life.

Your mountains clad with scented pines,
The ancient olive groves;
Ever-changing fields of vines,
All nature in repose.

The torrid heat of noon-day sun,
Turquoise shining sea,
Kings' tombs, mosaics, burial mounds,
A cliff-top Monastery.

Along the tortuous winding roads
Stand villages unknown,
'Midst orange groves and carob trees,
Where goats and donkeys roam.

This beauty hides a tragedy,
The desperate broken hearts
Of people living in a land,
So sadly torn apart.

Your wall-divided City,
Stands shimmering in the plain,
Old people born the other side,
Long to return in vain.

The young, their roots have yet to know,
But eternal hope is there,
One day will bring united land,
Freedom for all who care.

Meanwhile, the welcome stranger,
Is greeted with a smile,
To your land of myths and legends,
Fair Aphrodite's Isle.

Diana Jane Dean

Plymouth Resurgam (I Shall Rise Again)

From Celtic tribe and Saxon farms,
Plymouth became ships' port with arms.
Fourteen thirty-nine freedom's birth,
Borough, Mayor first on English earth.
Mariners made trade with New World,
Drake sailed the globe with flags unfurled.

The Spanish Armada was wrecked,
When Drake finished bowls and tide checked.
English fleet windward of Spaniards,
Fast fireships and scorching hazards,
Fought successful naval battle;
Destroying enemies significant chattel.

Tormented Christians sought refuge,
From harsh persecuting deluge.
They sailed for New World with pastor,
One ship unhappy disaster.
Plymouth gave them sound seamanship,
Pilgrims reached goal for true worship.

Plymouth chose William of Orange,
King with Parliament's keen challenge.
On River Tamar he built base,
With strong deep water dockyard space.
Devonport surged quickly ahead,
Now it is Europe's figurehead.

Plymouth, Britain's most blitzed city,
Rises now in entirety.
Largest city on south coast,
Ferries for Continent's keen host.
New Tamar road bridge to Cornwall,
Theatre Royal to enthral.

James Leonard Clough

The Night Ferry To Caen

The ship glides darkly on, the wavelets dance:
A British army is invading France.
Behold, the vanguard of our Middle Class
In camouflage with sunscreen and dark glass.
Those jutted chins each Frenchman will perturb -
Intent on massacring each native verb.
The tortured vowel they'll strangulate on sight;
The h goes missing at first sign of fight.
The present tense: its use alone abounds,
Whilst corpses of pluperfects lie in mounds.

The French with guns in each Réserve de Chasse
Believe they've reached a really sad impasse,
For as they shoot each sorry burbling lark,
Or any wren or robin in the park
(To form the base of terrine or of stew,
Transformed by madame with a dab of roux),
Rings out the shrill command to halt toute suite,
In accent crisp from Cheltenham or Fleet:
A grim Tribunal's on inexorable way,
With members from the RSPCA.

Despairing French defend their culture's worth
Against those Anglo-Saxons from the North.
The hordes advance, monopolise le parking
And spend le weekend in le crowded camping.
The French complain and wave their hands about
Where Britons would just grumble or might shout.
No Frenchman finds the necessary word
Depicting strong emotion with sang froid.
In striving to discover the mot juste
The English language comes to rule the roost.

Ma foi, I've heard the French have come ashore
Some tens of thousand strong, or even more,
At Folkestone by some subterranean vent:
Attacks on Oxford Street are imminent!
We must devise une entente cordiale
Encouraged by some Pouvoir Mondial;
We'll even use some phrases from abroad
And visit friends with total bon accord.
With glass in hand and seated knee to knee
We'll know that every homme a deux patries.

    Robert Montgomery

A Traveller's Tale!

I've climbed the hills of Kathmandu
Thro' snow-capped mountain scene,
I've trod the dusty plains below
And India's millions seen.

I've watched the Bali sunset sink
In warm and wafting air;
In jungle and the Thailand Isles
What breathless beauty there!

I've been among the poor folk
Of China's teeming throng,
And crossed the sampanned harbour
Of the waters of Hong Kong.

I've climbed in heat up Ayres Rock
And *cooled* in Alice Springs
Bemused my hopping kangaroos
And where koalas cling.

Having trekked beneath the Southern Cross
To bleak Falklands did I go;
To loneliness and barrenness
And penguins in the snow.

I've breathed Arizona's desert air
And warmed beneath the sun;
In lovely California
Along silver beaches run.

I've watched the springboks leap so fast
On Africa's distant plain
Seen leopards, lions in the bush
All waiting for the rain.

Though I've never left these English shores like others have to roam
My nephews, nieces all have gone, and brought back the world to
                                        me - at home!

Mollie D Earl

Wild Flowers Of The Forests

Primroses in abundance
Cornflower sways in the gently breeze.
Field poppy shows its beauty
Red with a smiling face.
Skylarks singing in the glorious sunshine.
Fairy carpet of yellow buttercups
Mingles with wild orchids
For a companion.
As the crows pass by to roost,
Night turns to dusk.

Alan Hattersley

One With The Turf

Like an invisible cloud, stretching over the land, of Eire,
Is the friendly warm smell, of turf on the range.
This national treasure is the soul of the land,
Perhaps though it's Bono form the rock and roll band.
Others say 'Guinness', 'The Blarney' or 'The book of Kelles',
They may have a point to a certain degree.
But this natural resource outweighs them by far.
Turf is the fuel through from Cork to Armagh.
It keeps the range warm and heats up the room,
The range does the cooking so people are fed,
It heats up the water so you can keep clean,
Turf doesn't cost much, do you know wha' I mean?
Turf's never ending, it comes from 'the Bog',
And that is quite big begad and also quite deep.
Bogs are all over Ireland, the north and the south,
It's also called 'Peat' if 'Turf' won't fit your mouth.
Turf on the range has a 'homely' smell, it makes you want to stay,
In Ireland the welcome's warm, the accent's great,
It's not too far from Brum.
Now that I have sold it well,
You'll *all* just have to come.

D Sawyer

The Times Have Changed

The times they have changed so much
Changed so much we all say
That with many of the old ways
Have gone the rule of good luck.

The times they have changed so much
Just changed beyond what is ok
No longer can just any one
Speak a lot to get his way.

The times they have changed so much
How can we change with it
For it is changing all the time
This world in which we live.

Keith L Powell

Beirut 1963

City beautiful in sunlit robe
And guarded by her watching, shifting seas.
So sometimes silver mingling, half real,
As interchanging, silent coves they probe.

The ancient city dreams towards Europe
Seeming in a slightly twilight mood.
Phoenician quinqueremes transmute to steel
As jewelled planes surmount the heliotrope.

See now how in the clouds of olive mist,
The tantalising city can't resist
To wear her evening dress of sparkling bronze.
A million teardrops glisten in their throngs.
Towards the velvet midnight let us tread.
Towards the teardrops - softly - let us tread.

Elizabeth Stephens

Sphinx

Scattered avenues of sphinx's line ancient southern walkways
From here to there Karnak to Luxor the triumphal march
The Festival of Opet and the Great Amun
Garlanded processions alive with mirth
Celebrations echoing back at us
As if the noise had seeped into the earth
Row upon row of proud sphinx's proclaim their worth.

Travel northwards in time through desert and delta
Glimpse the horizon and stop to catch your breath
For there in all majesty and splendour . . . the great Sphinx
Once target practice for Napoleon's army,
And did Cleopatra drape herself across your paws I wonder
As the mighty Caesar looked on?
Damaged, eroded, photographed, sketched and painted
Posed upon and passionately paraded in front of and around.
Secrets, lies, intrigues, chambers hidden from view
Now jealously guarded with incorruptible wisdom (we hope)
Argued and discussed at length about - this mighty magnificent
Monument is worshipped and adored.

However old you are great Sphinx
You remind us of our ancient past
And, as magnificent as you are
Inspiring wonder on the grand scale
Each time I look upon your form
I catch my breath . . .

Elaine Edgar

43

Cherveix Cubas

Near the church in Cherveix Cubas
There's a lantern of the dead
Of the eleventh century
(Or so I've heard it said).
If you drive to Cherveix Cubas
You will find when you arrive
That the shops along the village street
Are very much alive.

There's a wine shop on the corner
Just opposite the post,
But the little village bakery's
The one we use the most.

Inside that shop there is a sign
Which we have often seen,
'Please do not touch the bread
In the interests of hygiene.'
So when we choose our crusty loaf
And pass it with our francs
Madame wraps it round the middle
And returns it with her thanks.

There's a butcher and a pharmacist,
A coiffurist for the head,
But the shop we use each morning
Is where Madame sells her bread.

There's a shop that's full of trinkets
Where we buy our cartes postales,
And the grocer and green grocer
Who sells newspapers as well.
There's a hotel bar and restaurant,
A surgery for the vet
But since we have no animals
We haven't been there yet.

There's no sign of undertaker,
No chapel for the dead
But while Cubas has a baker
We'll enjoy our daily bread,
And when we praise our Maker
We'll give thanks for tasty bread.

Ken French

Oxford

I look out upon you;
nightmare of loneliness
dark and fading dreams;
all hope is swallowed
in your powerful,
defeating path;
you despise happiness.

Benn Raymond

India

In the glow from an early universe
I dress my kiss in your beard
India
I am but a grain of rice in your pudding
Absorbing the rays of a full moon
India
In your youngest of children
I see an adults toil
India
You are a bitch with too many puppies
A peacock with not enough feathers
India
Your streets so pungent with sewers and sweets
Henna, incense, oils and spice
India
I have travelled through you
You have travelled through me
India
I have milked your holy cow
Bucket between my knees trying not to spill
India
In an effort to understand I realise
True understanding requires no effort

Janice Whitlock

Weymouth

With siren-like songs, it summons me,
Tempestuous or calm, my siren, the sea,
Sultry and stormy it beckons me,
With untold longing I long for the sea.

Landlocked I linger but long for to hear,
The songs of that siren that seems to be near,
To feel the salt breeze so cold and so sere,
That was always my solace always my cheer.

Once more I'll return come what may,
O how I long for that wonderful day!
To gaze once again on Weymouth bay,
And walk oft along the old Roman way.

Roger Caswell

The Enchanted City

As we arrive at the Gard du Nord,
There is magic in the air,
Our taxi amidst that famous roar,
An atmosphere so rare!

The Champs-Elysees with all its charm,
Or is it spoilt - no never never,
Holds us always in its palm,
The perfect boulevard - same as ever!

We stroll along beside the Seine,
Then to the Mona Lisa,
In the Bois de Boulogne - sans any rain,
The Eiffel Tower so tall and straight - no Pisa!

The Arc de Triomphe - its eternal flame,
So dignified and moving,
This City still so much the same,
All beauty and so soothing.

Notre Dame in all its splendour,
Stands out against the sky,
A City enough to make you purr,
Perhaps even weep or cry!

The restaurants of every style,
With food so rare and renowned,
Quite worthy of that extra mile,
No chance to shed a pound!

Romance is always in the air,
For the young and old alike,
Everywhere you look - behold a pair,
Poor Cupid - nowhere else to strike!

It holds a place in all our hearts,
This City so supreme,
For Paris surely heads the charts,
Fulfilment of every dream!

Jill M Ronald

Teide's Crater

World apart more moonscape than earth
Molten monoliths inhabit this place,
Rock Titans stand tall, menacing,
Grotesque monsters stride mouths gaping,
As local legend portrays
God's finger granite-like points upward,
Afar fairy-like castles
Blend to the sky line.
All is desolate. Awe-inspiring.

What massive force
Rocked, tossed Teide
In seventeen hundred and seven?

Patricia Weitz

West Country Blues

Radstock is a colder place now.
Darkened and dreamless.
The jet black no longer trundles
in trucks
on tracks
of rusty flaking orange.
The harsh wind no longer
etches dust into the grey brick cottages.
The awesome piles and batches
are early summer green these days
no longer malevolently proud.
Abandoned industry - denying its history.
Radstock is a colder place now.

Ade Macrow

Beautiful Torbay

And I have journeyed abroad a few times,
Nothing ever beats coming home I find.
Because home is the borough of Torbay,
Beauty outstanding, what more can I say.
Has the best of two areas of beauty,
Can visit the countryside, or the sea.

For both have a special place in my heart,
Miss them, when on my travels I depart.
All the seasons in the bay, bring their own joys,
Endless hours watching nature I employ.
I'd never emigrate from this county,
Where would I find like settings to move me?

S Mullinger

My Ethiopian Holiday (Late 1980s)

Five weeks in Ethiopia spent with my son,
Proved to be a memorable and exciting one,
At Holetta I stayed in beautiful terrain,
Eight thousand feet up in scenery like the highlands, and no rain.
Addis Ababa itself had a communist stance,
Lenin's statue and sloganed archways I saw at a glance.
The African parliament, a building very grand.
Just the way Haile Selassie had it all planned.
Its stained glass windows portraying the life
Of Africa before came communist onslaught and strife.
The unusual carved stone lion of Judah one can see,
A reminder of Ethiopian culture when its people were free.
Modern skyscrapers and hotels, alongside the hovel,
Just a one roomed tin shack, in which to grovel.
Native butchers shops, meat by roadside displayed
To dust, petrol fumes and flies, not exactly first grade.
To children, from an early age, English is taught in school,
Surprising to find this should be the rule
A Sue Ryder and Cheshire home perched on lonely mountainside,
A marathon race being run, funds for orphans to provide.
By city roadside, funeral tents are erected and stay for a week
For relatives and mourners to meet, as solace they seek.
Emperor Meneliks abode, his regalia and possessions on display.
Jewelled coronation robes, three tiered crown, in dazzling array.
Visiting fields of Tef, the grain of the nation,
My son improving crops to prevent future starvation.
Staying overnight at Rift Valley Game Park, where I saw
Many rare animals, baboons and exotic birds galore.
Visiting a famous leprosy hospital where patients learn
To spin, weave and embroider, a living to earn.
Seeing statue of St George on main thoroughfare,
Strange to think with Ethiopia, our patron saint we share.

Invitation to tea at British Embassy, an unexpected treat,
In palatial surroundings, an idyllic retreat.
Going to their garden party to celebrate Armistice Day,
A lovely way to spend final day of my holiday.
Into my late seventies, I was sorry to return,
One is *never* too old to live and to learn

Kathleeen Jones

Koh Samui-Thailand

(Dedicated to the memory of Joss, RIP. The special trips on Tangaroa.
The late husband of Claude and father to Edward and the baby.
A friend to Ryk and Sharon, John, and many more)

The world is still
The night is dark.
The air is warm
Upon the sands.

I'm upon the beach
I can hear the sea.
The lapping waves
Upon the sands.

Above the palms
Higher still the stars.
A perfect night
Upon the sands.

The temple built
High on the hill.
Big Buddha looks
Down on the sands.

A perfect day
A restful night.
Just count your gifts
Upon the sands.

  Christine Webster

Wartime In London

When bombs were falling all around
We spent our nights down under ground.
We heard the aircraft zooming by
Dropping danger from the sky.
Each day we came into the light,
Our roads were then a sorry sight,
With craters here and craters there
And bricks and rubble everywhere.
Each day we tidied up and then
The following night it happened again.
Night after night to the shelter we fled,
Life seemed to be either at work or in bed.
The shelter was down in our garden quite deep,
So after a while, we found we could sleep.
Ignoring the noises of planes and big guns
We stayed there until the next day had begun.
At last came the time we felt it was right
To sleep in the house and have a good night.
Our comfortable beds had never felt so good
After sleeping for months on blankets on wood.
Remembering that time of worry and fear
It's hard to believe our London's still here.
We Britons are tough, we rebuilt our town
And no-one can keep a true Londoner down.

Kathleen Abbott

A Coach Tour

Off on a coach tour for the day
To view the sights along the way
Up past Balmoral, no Queen did see
Then we travelled on, up through Glenshee.

Our destination was Blair Castle
The imposing home of the Duke of Athol
With many sights for us to stare
He's got his private army there.

Then to Pitlochry the shops to ogle
With prices that set the mind to boggle
Their public loos as clean as any
But they charge ten pence to spend a penny.

Through Dunkeld, past Mieklour's Beechy hedges
As nearer home our coach now edges
And when at last we reach the station
We disembark with desperation.

Union Terrace toilets now a must
To empty bladder before it bursts
For in Aberdeen you see
They dinna charge ye for a *pee.*

Douglas Parley

Littlehampton

A shell, a pebble, and a strand of weed,
A calm, mild, cloudy day and a still sea.
The waves wash in and fill with silent speed
The castles in the sand - and there I see
The years dissolve, the firm impacted sand
Give way to the onrushing tide of time -
However long the road, how firm our stand,
Our aging years move on apace to frost and rime
Where Charon waits to ferry us across
The River Styx. But no we shall not stay,
Nor looking at the past - bewail the loss
Of energetic youth, nor sail away
To Avalon's sweet isle across the mere;
Together we shall be, forever here.

John Stanbridge

58

Fuerteventura: Sea, Dunes, Lava-Flow

Upon the beach crash sapphire waves
And fuse with emerald stirred with sand;
The restless sea unfurling raves
And beats against the fragile land.

The dunes stretch back into the dry
And empty wilderness behind,
Where long-dead sea-shells scattered lie
And grain-husk fossils one can find.

And colonizing seedlings here
To desert dust with nerve hold fast;
Some then as scrubby plants appear
Or spindly trees that shadows cast.

Some manage to come into flower,
As if a future they descry;
Plump caterpillars, though, devour
Their luckless siblings doomed to die.

So wander up and down the dunes,
Which Nature underneath one's feet
With wind-packed wavelets now festoons:
The silent solitude's complete.

The scrub encroaches ever more
When you approach the lava-flow:
Now see, where torrents ceased to pour,
A wall of chunks dropped there below.

No longer glowing with the fire,
These rocks still sport a coloured sheen,
For, as more lichens they acquire,
They're gold and lemon, ochre, green.

Within the duneland's ample sweep
The wind whips up a sandy haze,
Behind which distant islands sleep
Whose charm arrests the dreamer's gaze.

Nearby is Lobos, earthy, brown,
Grey Lanzarote far off lies,
In dark blue waters settling down,
While inky ribbons brush the skies.

From gold to pink the light now shifts,
And setting sun plays hide-and-seek:
Behind the large dark clouds in drifts
Like dragons' puffs the small clouds peek.

The sea's now pale and icy blue,
While fiery clouds the sky contest
To swirl and blaze till sucked down through
The stern horizon in the west.

    Anne Sanderson

Evening Abroad

The gently swaying tops of many lofty palms
look down on endless rows of hardy little vines,
while simple Arab chanting sounds like broken psalms
and up on high the silver of a young moon shines.

Out there in the distance lie dark blue jagged hills,
breaking up the skyline; vermilion - tinted yet,
while on the farmhouse roof with loudly rattling bills
ghostly storks are courting in weird silhouette.

A O Jones

A Garden Full Of Praise And Prayer

I've walked the paths of fragrant air,
A place to dream and stroll,
A garden full of praise and prayer
Where pleasure soothes the soul.

I've seen the hands of gentleness
Move with artistic skill,
While beauty holds and seems to bless
The garden and the hill.

Above the pool with blur or wing
A dance for Summer's day,
A damselfly with joy to bring,
Performance and display.

Then its reflection caught my eye,
Its friend and counterpart,
Synchronously while dancing by
Creation moved my heart!

In nearness to the waterfall
What love tranquillity!
Where nature sings and wraps her shawl
My tears fell silently.

So garden touched by grace and charm
My heart I've left with you!
For you are Eden blessed by calm
Where angels paint the view!

Peter James O'Rourke

Howrah City Express

Choking, sweltering, strangling
Cattled human nature,
Locked, shocked, mocked
Sirens scream.
Teaming rotten sweated bodies
Cooking, baking, writhing,
Money, money rushed life,
Shoe shiners, beggars
Pickpockets swiped,
Now you see it
Now you don't.
Kamla lebu quench your thirst,
Thumbs up, cola, chaai,
Murder the furnaced heat.
In strangled Calcutta summer.
Hustled, rushed disturbed,
Like ants see them scarper
Children clutched,
Walk on people,
Howrah globed India
Disorganised disarray
Think fast, think

Darkness, silence, sleep
Tread the human carpet,
Dawn cracks beckon.
Rush rush, faster faster
Run catch your life.

Another day
Another morning
Howrah city.

Rita Pal

An Evening That Dreams Are Made From

The sun turned the sky to gold then sank into a sea of fire,
The restaurant on the beach had become a magic place on that
sensual August night,
Toni and Rick were laying down the blues cool,
Candle light and promises were reflected in amber eyes.
This was sorcery an enchanted atmosphere that captivated senses,
I was spellbound by this vision of splendour before me whose smile
turned me into a prince,
Whose touch revealed my poverty,
I knew my future would only exist in her memory of the dispossessed,
I was just a guest in the company of supremacy.

William C Thomas

Through The Lochs To The Top

To be together, anywhere at all
That's what we desired and got
Travelling to Inverness no less
To play his men on their jobs up there
I too did travel in that old Post Office van
Double bed inside, 'twas great for the ride
From Glasgow we did go
In that old van we did love so
Cold winter nights, no problem to us
Hot water bottle filled from that old bus
Romance, heartache and sorrow
We lived for today, not for tomorrow
Love came to us in many ways
Above in a hay barn, with fags alight
Beneath the ferns trying to keep dry
Pitching a tent and then we did fly
A bull was on t'other side of the stream
Snorting and puffing for us to see
We ran like hell and left tent and all
And crept beneath a tarpaulin
To sleep and keep dry
One of the tales that is quite true
There are many more tales that I can tell you.

Sheila Wall

West Australia's Wild Flowers

To travel for hours and hours
Through wonderful shrubs and wild flowers,
Masses of beautiful colours to see
Stretched out on each side like the sea.

The expanse of trees, shrubs and flowers,
Their different shapes and colour overpowers,
It overwhelms you the first time you view
No gardener could believe that it's true.

The ocean colours are a wonderful sight
Beach colours vary, yellow to pure white,
Like surfers, in the waves, dolphins swim free
And wild flowers grow right down to the edge of the sea.

We are sure, as we've been there to see
Spring, in West Australia, we were lucky to be,
Now there is one thing left we must do
That is to tell West Australia; we love you!

To you, Eric and Diana, brother and sister we tell
Your friends are now our friends as well,
You took us north and south, during our stay
Over your friendly, colourful, vast country, WA

Your hospitality we can never repay,
If and ever, please come here to stay,
Do not hesitate, whatever you do
As together, we really love you.

Denis and Mavis Constance

Karnak

Great pillars of stone that reach up to heaven,
Ornate carvings adorn the top of lotus flowers and papyrus grass,
Obelisks erect, cast long shadows in the sun,
Monuments strewn around in ruin, of great men
Where priests had worshipped at their feet,
The sacred lake shimmering in the midday heat,
The dark cool place of the holy of holies
Rituals performed there no more,
The almighty temple of Karnak in Luxor.

Vannesa Fitzgerald

Round The World

To take a trip around the world
So many sights to see
So many wonders that enfold
By land, by air, by sea.
Ancient Egypt, has its pharaohs,
The Sphinx of history,
On then to the wilds of Africa
It's Table Mountain, Gold Coast, lions,
Plus that grand old beast, the elephant.
Joys in life that all must see.
There's ancient Venice with its gondolas,
Its canals, St Martins Square,
Its Bridge of Sighs and glassware wonders.
A must in life to see
Visit next the Isle of Sicily,
Its volcano Etna, a focal point that all must see.
Then there's the mystic of the Orient.
Cycled taxis everywhere, so many two wheeled cycles,
Bells ringing everywhere.
Holland has its grand canals for travel anywhere,
A place to take your camera, show all at home
That you were there.
Then there Russia with its Kremlin,
The Arc de Triomphe of Paree.
So many wonders of our world, too many to relate,
My pen is running out of ink, time is very late.
Please bear with me if I have missed
Your favourite place in life.
The wonders of our ancient world
Are to numerous to relate.

Leslie Rushbury

Roof Of The World

Beneath sails of the Tibetan moon
cares melted into butter lamps
in misted gold
in foothills chanting
in soft rain praying
to life, to life
So precious
where love, respect for all that lives
walk hand in hand
and winds call lama, lama
Where sun storms blanket mountains
embracing land
a wilderness so close to heaven
the roof of the world
in burnt orange sky
a million diamond pips
to frosted clouds
a million grasses whisper
wild yes wild we are
free yes free we are
nature blooms in glory
as prayer flags chorus
another Tibetan day

Hazel Houldey

Niagara Falls

Picture a river,
    rocky and rainbow kissed,
while riding white foam
    on the 'Maid of the Mist'.
Blue plastic capes,
    all flapping and swollen,
filling our boat which was
    tossing and rolling.

She was skilfully steered
    thru' bright shining waters.
In wonder we stared,
    as the magic had caught us.
Just awed by the power of
    those wild tumbling walls,
I was struck by the splendour
    of the Niagara Falls!

Sonja F Mills

US Highway

I dream of and English garden
small and gentle and kind
green green meadows and soft rain falling
with sun not far behind
in a low grey sky shot over with silver
soft as a pigeon's breast
low on the woods where branches whisper
when wind comes out of the west

The wide wide skies of Kansas
have a beauty all their own
the red rocks of Colorado
and smooth hills of velvet brown
folding over towards the west
with a strong and rhythmic motion
falling away to the rocky coast
and the wide Pacific ocean

Each land is God's own country
for those who have tilled the soil
learning to love and to nurse it
through seasons of patient toil
yet surely the Lord was angry
when he tore the canyons apart
and painted the rocky mountains
with blood from the Saviour's heart.

For it's hard and cruel in the Bad Lands
and cold on the mountain pass
there is nothing to eat in the desert
where sand drifts over the grass
where sterile winds from the sierra
blow hotly over the plain
but the warm west winds of England
bring beauty and richness and rain

The men who have conquered this country
are stronger and better than I
they have learned to limit its anger
yet weakly I wish to die
in a gentle land where grass is green
softly to cover my rest
to be washed anew in cool clean rain
when the wind comes out of the west

Anne Stevens

Harrow Weald, Middlesex

In 'Environs of London' author Thorne,
When hastily describing Harrow Weald,
Some sixty years before TV was born,
Said it had little but a timber yield.

Young Trollope trod uneasy paths of old
Now neatly made up into busy roads,
And Daniel Dancer danced upon his gold
Where proudly stands a ribbon of abodes.

The Blackwell residence, The Kiln, still stands.
For years the Kiln was worked by Bodimeades.
The City, fourteen cottages, housed hands.
Now one remains: the others gone to seed.

Eighteen-twenty-nine saw Crosse and Blackwell
Together come to feed those many mouths.
Their products in those handy tins stack well,
To satisfy, on supermarket shelves.

The lake where Gilbert drowned is now a puddle,
Grimsdyke in which he lived is an hotel,
Where ancient trees once stood brick buildings huddle,
And people come from far away to dwell.

A spate of building has erased the green,
Desire for progress pulled the Smithy down,
With Wealdstone having sprung up in between,
The market stretches through to Harrow Town.

But best is green belt land at Harrow Weald,
Land that Nature fashioned for our pleasure.
We have the Common and the open field.
Let no man nor woman steal that treasure.

F G Ward

Ko Phi Phi

The island's sky streaked red and gold
Under a burning sun.
Calming waters gently caressed the shore
With the trawler on the horizon
Silhouetted against green and craggy rocks.
An island of perfume,
Of flowers and palm trees,
Small, wooden beach huts,
Stretches of white sand.
The cliffs a danger,
A thrill, a beauty,
Eternity.
The island of love,
Of moonlight and dancing.
Firelight on the beach,
A midnight and balmy warmth.
And beneath that sky
It was I who danced,
I who sang,
I who loved,
And it was I who left
Perhaps never to return
Except in my memories - a thousand times
Phi Phi - an island - my dream.

Clare King

Les Brugues

Trees of every shape, size and colour
Intermingle one with the other,
As far as the eye can see.
Finches, Hoopos, Woodpeckers, in colourful plumage,
Kites, Black Buzzards glide on high,
All singing their beautiful song.
The Red Squirrel races across the lawn,
Lizards darting hither and thither
Up the walls, over the stones,
All viewed from the terrace,
Edged with trays, tubs, of flowers beneath hanging baskets full.
Laurzette in the distance, high on top of a hill
Spilling over and down the rocks,
The quiet, peace, beauty, you catch your breath,
Gaze spellbound, nature at its very best.
Step inside the cool tiled floors,
Wide, high ceilinged, spacious rooms.
Perfumed air wafts through open windows,
Gentle music in every room.
All is calm, all is Les Brugues in all its glory.

M Andrews

Caister-On-Sea

Our village is a moonscape with car park.
A desert of empty skull-like disposable cartons,
A hungry wind sinks its teeth into the ochre sands.
Our village is a reservation of garages and poker-faced drivers.
Some still breathe to prove they are alive.
Our village is ugly without reason or cause.
No heavy industry to blame or dark Satanic mills,
Just acre upon acre of half-pint dwellings,
Their owners grey, pink faces framed inside plastic windows;
Portraits in a waste land that I once knew.

Laurence De Calvert

The Yearly Disaster

Here we go, it's that time of year again,
We're all looking forward to visiting Spain,
Getting the kids organised with a bit of a pain,
Loaded the bags in a taxi said goodbye to the rain,
At the airport waited hours for our plane,
Bored youngsters, I thought they were going to drive me insane.

Eventually at our destination unloaded the baggage in the rain,
The hotel wasn't all it was cracked up to that was plain,
A waiter spilt wine on my best dress now there's a nasty stain,
The sun came out and I enjoyed exploring many a picturesque lane,
I sent postcards but to sound happy my efforts were all in vain,
Sunburnt, miserable and broke I will never leave home again.

Well not until next year anyway.

Ann Woolven

The Music For All

So many words, songs, psalms, writ
New or ancient in stone or papyrus
With pictures or artless
The words fit.

In poetry all told from men in times
Grown old, lyrics modernising
Writing their frail message
Testimonies knit

From religious wisdom to caustic wit
In rhythms that do exist
From mortals, an unseen guide
In popular hit

To any mysticism we will not
Understand. From the grand to infantile
The volumes now persist
Will always sit

Upon the endless shelves or in museums
Where inspiration must die or live. A
Joyous road with great message or grief for all
Until the way is light.

John Amsden

Night Train

Darkness shot through with sudden slivers of gold,
Night train Riga to Moscow clearing its throat,
The wheels a clicking out rhythm fold on fold
Of soft steady noise. Insomniacs we float
In a nutshell; outside the night, the world.

Time passes heavily like the beat of blood
Pushed through the heart. A frayed fur-cap curled
Like Mandleshtam's, in his pocket, hands ice cold,
Remembered on looking at the landscaped snow.
Unlike him to a safe destination we move
Into daybreak - Tomorrow, white Moscow.

Lit by a sudden platform we dissolve
In multicoloured lights, a mingled glow
Of amethyst and amber, red and green,
Then back into jet dark, rocked to and fro
In the warm womb, of what? Our speeding train.

Tolstoy, you should have been born in this hour:
Softly-lit empty corridors windowing
Outside, your Russia, glowing like a Stone Flower,
Passes us swept by winter's winnowing,
Different yet the same, we almost breathe in

Your smile with the chill air, your wondering gaze
White as blizzard, taut as a stripped birch tree,
Stood back against the steppe, in misted haze
Suspended, outwaiting the Spring's return -
After the thaw, your Russia brave and free,
And that which you alone could shape and know,
The Russia of Yesterday - tomorrow *now*.

Alan C Brown

Touring In The Loire Valley

We left the seventh century church at Savonnieres
Where prayers have been ascending for twelve centuries;
The car jerked round a mediaeval street corner
Scattering the masses of facts in my mind.
I breathed in the aromatic Loire air,
When, like characters in a school play
Three young girls stepped on the scene,
Bronzed, dark-eyed, in joyous colours.
What grace, what animation, beauties all,
Baskets on their arms, one crowned a dark head.
'Gypsies' said a Sister, cold-splashing my fantasy.
Then a hand shyly stretched in a begging gesture;
I expected my hostesses to drop in a coin,
But all minds were on the car -
We were at a sticky point -
We moved along. I hope a smile from an
Unveiled head conveyed a flashing warmth
To those children from the smooth south;
Who can tell how they enhanced my day?
While memories of chateaux and churches are indistinct
Their calm freshness remains, richly endearing.

Mary Frances Mooney

Breathe Close To Me

Breathe close to me, and all your love-thoughts tell.
Drowsy and warm, perfumed from musky sleep,
Your body's balm crushed to my face I keep;
Its feminine and all-enchanting spell
Casts out despair, and stirs my blood as well.
Over my senses your quick fingers creep
(Oh, at their touch, oh, how my pulses leap!)
Breathe close to me, and feel my passion swell:
Embrace, each intimate part adore and kiss;
With amorous sighs enjoy each inhalation
And, through our carnal ecstasy and bliss,
Achieve, in love, a spiritual exaltation.
Except like this, held childlike to your breast,
From desolate loneliness there is no rest.

Bernard Brown

The Fuhrer

She died with his name in her mouth
One day they would know the truth
What she'd endured would now cease
It was over now, she had peace

She was one of many in the camp
Life to death, like a flickering lamp
There was nothing left to try
They'd used her up, she was ready to die

Liberated in death
His name, on her last intake of breath

Sue White

Friends In The Dark

I don't know how to express my love,
My love for you my Lord above.

I know I must, I must speak out,
But I just don't know what to talk about.

I want to speak, I want to shout,
But what to say, and what about.

You mean so much in my life today,
And yet I don't know what to say,

I need courage, I must be bold,
I need to feel your loving hold.

What to say, and when to say,
What to bring them to, and who are they.

All these things I ask Thee Lord,
Time is what I can't afford.

I hand my friends all up to you,
Guide me Lord, help me work it through.

R Barnett

Sweet Dreams

Stars are out
Night has come
Tiny tots asleep
In tiny cots

And little buns
With puffy cheeks
Dream softly sweet
The sandman's gift

Parents blissful slumber
Babies silently snooze
Toddlers playing peeps
With baby mice

Moon smiles down
Clearly cheery night
The cities safe
Now, good night!

Kevin C Dwane

Always There

Always there for hubby,
Always there for kids,
Always there for mother,
Always there for sisters,
Who's there for me?
No one I can tell,
No one's there when I need,
Now I need a rest,
Always there for someone,
For everyone but me,
I do wish someone,
Would be there just for me,
No there is no one,
And there never will be,
Always there for someone
For everyone but me.

   J Jones

Not For The Faint-Hearted

We should be thinking of how to bring a little excitement to those
who are not so mobile.
There is, of course, help to get around and to assist movement all the
while.
But they only operate in slow motion which does not encourage
adrenaline to flow.
If they could be adjusted I'm sure it would be welcome by some
friends that we know.
To imagine yourself at Brands Hatch is too much to expect.
But if that wheelchair could be speeded up and yet treated with
respect.
It would call for skills that could eventually aim at an advanced class.
Presenting a kind of challenge with perhaps a prestigious award if
they
pass.
The stairlift provides essential travel as it glides slowly on its way.
Whereas if set to whiz up and down it would make somebody's day.
The bed that is adjustable could also provide excitement and
distraction.
If it were set to move up and down quickly with unlimited action.
And then there is perhaps talent in the supermarket - there should be
a section for shopping rage.
For some steer those trolleys skilfully with no restriction on age.
This of course should be read as its meant to be - with tongue in
cheek!!
But I'm sure many of our unfortunate friends have a sense of
humour, that they required to get them through the week.

Reg Morris

High Mountains

You cannot climb high mountains
Before you've walked low ground
And on the road to wisdom
No short cut can be found.
Have courage in adversity
You will not strive in vain
There never was a rainbow
Without a fall of rain.

William Price

In The Context Of Things

The bend in the river,
I remember it all too well:
Dartmoor, June 20th 1984.
That's when you said it's over.

It didn't come as such a shock.
The beauty of the scenery
I was surrounded with
somehow tempered it.
Besides I'd half expected as much.
It can happen to any of us.

You continued to speak.
I could hear your voice
in the background,
but somehow I was absorbed by something else,
something more significant perhaps
than our little troubles.

So what if we were falling apart,
going our separate ways.
So what if you'd found someone else.
I had the wind and the trees.
That was all I needed.
You were almost trivial
in the context of things.
Anyway, if I'm honest,
it was someone else I loved.

I wish I'd had it
somewhere in my heart
to make you the one,
but I could not.
So I left you there
in the rain and the mud,
and with it, your last hope
of true happiness,
for within a year
you'd been dumped yourself.
Funny how things turn around.
Funny indeed how they turn out.

Andy Botterill

A Promise

Heartache, loss, tears, pain and sorrow
To know we have yet to face a tomorrow
Is this all there is, to the life God gives
Is this all we get for the short time one lives . . .
Not many words of comfort, a line quoted from a friend
Things we don't understand down here,
Will all be explained, in the end . . . '

  J Tryhorn

Terminus

The night was dark and stormy.
Bitter with rain and sleet.
An old vagrant, shoulders hunched
against the cold, stumbling along
by the railroad track. Footsore
and weary, with leaden feet.
Pausing by a few discarded sleepers.
He sits down for a while, to rest, and
reflect.
Upon his head, an old hat, brim turned up
at each side, now stained, and discoloured
like flotsam, swirling along with the tide.
He remembers the woman, who shared his bed.
The happy years, since the day they were wed.
He thinks of the night she died. Gone was
the once firm link.
Bereft, weighed down with his sorrow. He couldn't
cope and turned to the drink.
Friends that he knew, all drifted away.
Forlorn, and sad, he curses the day.
Unaware that his time has come.
They found him in the early light of dawn.
A broken old wreck, laying in a puddle. Flat
on his back. The old hat, that once was his pride,
half full of rain water, close by his side.
No more will he hear the whistle of a train,
or sit by a campfire, sharing a bottle of cheap
wine. For the old hobo tis the end of the line.

John Murray

Ormeau 12th Of July

New pressure appears a protest
Years of watching waiting
Leaning against railings talking
Ormeau 12th of July 1999

Usual response to questions
Single new place near the sky
Others around, sty clean
Collision course begins ends

Marching Orangemen British
Both sides in our imagination
From one side of Belfast
Barricades Ormeau 12th of July

S M Thompson

Just Peace

If I could have a wish
I know what it would be
For peace all over the planet
A world wartorn free
I'd wish for all the peoples
To come together as one
No wars, no anger, no hatred
Just peace for everyone

Alan Green

Valentine's Day Passed By

I waited for the Postman
But the Postman didn't come.
I wanted to get some roses
But the roses had had no sun.
I sat beside the telephone
I didn't get a call.
So what did I get for Valentines?
Basically . . . Naf all.

A card with hearts and flowers on
Or one just making fun.
A soppy rhyme or limerick
Or a dirty, sexy one.
A small lovers token is all I need
To show my love is well.
Did I get this from my Valentine . . .
Did I? Like bloomin' hell.

I have a sweet tooth for chocolate
And I just adore silky underwear.
I just wanted a sign of affection
Someone to show they care.
I have not seen Cupids' arrow
If he shot then he sadly missed.
Another day, no special Valentine . . .
No card . . . no flowers . . . unkissed

Robert Harris

Motherless

Not knowing my mother, she died at my birth
My fathers role was two parents as well as a nurse.
He was so kind and gentle, I being the apple of his eye,
Surrounded by his many talents, so spoiled was I.
Relatives would scold and lecture when they visited us,
Father made so many excuses, many then he snubbed,
Interfering in our lives, he to me would complain
As he sat me on his knee so happy were we again.

Growing up with one parent and he being male
Presents a lot of questioning of him I prevail.
T'was alright in the nursery, the infants and junior mixed,
Now it comes to senior girls, we are both in a fix.
I had never heard of periods, I could not consult my dad,
The other girls laughed and jeered, life became so sad.
My teacher called me aside and explained what I had to do,
Now in private solitude I worked all out and all is proven true.

From dad I held no secrets as embarrassed I revealed the shock.
He knew an adolescents body, especially girls, changed a lot.
He understood my feelings as our love grew even stronger,
I became the new qualified head of this school,
My alma mater as I am fonder.
Dad by now was ailing fast and only I could care
It was difficult but I managed with home help and day care.
He passed away so peacefully one Sunday afternoon,
I had been reading to him as we sat there in the gloom.
I felt his hand suddenly grow cold and slip as I attempted to restore,
He looked so calm and as if sleeping as I silently closed the door.
Now all that is left are fond memories that I cherish and adore.

R D Hiscoke

Yearning

Happy birthday Susan and Gerry,
I'm sorry Mother I could not help
not meaning to offend
Just getting on with mundane tasks,
mundane tasks are everything.
One must have chores
clean the cooker and fix the bed,
and other things that cannot be fixed,
Everyday things we do by day
tire the weary bones,
a comfort and joy
maybe a plant needs water,
and you pour it on,
the water of life,
the joy of know,
it might flower,
a husband's dinner,
energy for an hour or two
tide him over a hard day,
sweep the floor
take away the dust
let in the light
open the door
a new morn
and thy head aches
Pray at mass on bended knee,
sometimes it touches the yearning heart,
Yearning for the grace of God.

Martina Joyce

Thank You

Whenever I am feeling low or down
You never fail me, you're always around.
Whatever the trouble, whatever the care,
You listen to me, you're always there
To give advice or lend an ear,
To hold my hand and calm my fears.
You help me in so many ways,
You get me through the troublesome days.
It's rare to find so true a friend.
Someone like you who backs me to the end.
Mere words simply cannot convey
Nor can they show in any way
How I appreciate all you do
And just how much I love you.

Sandra Thomas

Reality

The winds of time that come and go,
The trails of life are always on show.
Facing feats to bring some wealth,
As hazards repeats on your health.
Life and loves may be far away,
Peace of mind wanting to stay.
The voice reaches out just to touch,
Facing the future, is this too much?
Use your wisdom in your heart,
As money and friends can easily part.

Mary E Gill

Metamorphosis

For years I have desperately sought your approval.
Saying what I thought you wanted to hear.
Liking what you liked, I stopped seeing my friends,
whilst you controlled and manipulated me with fear.
I agreed with your views to save any argument,
only watching the programmes you wanted to see.
I lost my confidence and began to feel useless.
In front of your friends, you humiliated me.

Only by leaving could I take a step
back and see what you were doing to me.
Now to go forward, plan a new future, regain
self respect, make decisions, reclaim my dignity.
No longer useless with nothing to offer, now
I am stronger with views of my own,
and freedom to try new experiences, to say
what I feel and make my needs known.

Remember life is not a rehearsal, have confidence.
Don't be influenced by others or you will find
you are your own worst enemy, be happy.
You are your own person, with a fertile mind.
Be whatever you want to be. Stand up
for your beliefs. If you make a mistake
learn for the next time, without any regrets.
Live life to the full, you are unique.

Pamela Eldridge

Kosovo

Sadness is not
in words.
The heart is
fixed to death
with a large
hat pin.
The rain weeps,
but it cannot
cry enough
for the people.
The stench of hell
is in the air
not in Rome
or Paris
but in Kosovo.
Images will be replayed
until the film
is stored away.
Memories fade.
Hurt stays
especially when
the violin plays.

Tom Clarke

The Rhinestone Adventurer!

Oh I am the great adventurer
With me there's none to complete
I've stood on the top of Mount Everest
And smiled on the world at my feet!

I've battered my way thro' wild sandstorms
The desert has no terrors for me
Through the wild tangled verdure of forests
I have come out unscathed and free!

Wild tribes blow before me and acclaim
My prowess with sword and with spear.
Yes, when I lead them they are different men
With whom none can compete - far or near.

I rule many tribes and vast kingdoms
My realms stretch over the globe
And all nations they fear and they tremble too,
When I stand in my crown and my robe!

The storm tossed waves I face bravely
And dive to the oceans vast depth
I've seen all the wrecks in the vast oceans maw
From me no secrets are kept.

Now how you may ask can I do this -
I'll give you my secret, pray listen -
Seven pints of strong ale or whisky galore
And you'll fly from this dull prosaic prison!

In dreamland you will be a Titan,
Or politician with great acumen,
Or even the worlds greatest lover,
In dreams that come long after ten!

Alan Goodwin

For Just One Hour

There you stand above me
brooding, pensive, hair wind-blown,
you stare across the moors
like your thoughts are not your own.
You do not speak, or smile,
then suddenly your face I see,
a rugged creature, I long for you constantly.
Slowly, you engage my eyes
you descend from where you stand,
dressed in a cape of jet,
you beckon me, with one strong hand.
I'm drawn to you so forcefully,
until I feel your fingertips,
held to your manly frame,
passion burning, from your lips.
The kiss needs no accompaniment
words can't justify its voice,
I'm lost within the moment
decisions fade, I have no choice.
I want you, how I want you,
a prayer that's answered intense its power,
alive with passion I've craved for,
be mine Heathcliff, if only for just one hour . .

Sherran Clark

Tranquillity

As the evening sun sinks out of sight
Leaving behind its golden streaks across the sky,
Another glorious day is forecast before onset of night
As the heralds of the day slowly die.
This tranquil beauty surely is the messenger of peace:
Who can deny the glory of God's creation?
It is there for eyes to see and who can cease
To wonder at the mystery and inspiration
Of the unknown God who gives so much love.
What has man done to spoil this image?
May the ethereal, winged beauty, the dove
Find its way into this unsettled age.

Patricia Kennett

I Was Born After The War

I was born after the War. I never knew what my father saw.
My mother died when I was small, I had to go off to school.
I was born after the War. My father never told me about it at all.

He didn't mention how Coventry, London, Dresden and Vietnam were
                                                        bombed.
How he and my mother had to hide on the Undergrounds.

I guess he got on with his life, went to work, but then he died.
I was born after the War. I never heard my father really mention it
                                                        . . . at all.

T C Maltby

The New Covenant

The Host was made by human hands,
The corn grew from the sod,
But O! the life within the mould
Is of the Living God.

O marvellous humility!
He dwells with us again;
He lives - the everlasting Lord,
Tabernacled among men.

Daphne Foreman

Plastic Destiny

Why an artificial noun?
Why an object of obscurity?
Multi-coloured, multi-lingual, multi-purpose
even multi-storied . . .
many faces, many facets, many guises
like a bowl, brush, comb, cassette-case
deodorant, flower vase, dustpan and brush
pedal-bin, swing-bin, litter bin . . .
I wear a mask in this ethereal echo
longing like Eleanor Rigby to be free
once put before an oil painting I owned obscurity
paled into insignificance, paled like faded wallpaper
that everyone forgets until needed
my destiny is only a recycling box like me
hollow, mundane, artificial
untreasured like a crystal cut glass vase
another noun, dead existence lives on
until I have served my purpose
to hug living daffodils, to contain water,
wash the wear-and-tear from weary feet
crying inside for recognition
like the portrait painted oil
in pride of place over mantelpiece.
Onyx statues starkly cold in contrast
and the round gilded clock mocks me
silvery spoons, knives, forks catch candlelit golden glow
reflecting in white wine glasses and clear blue crockery
I am a wine bottle opener; here for a transitory time
of vague nostalgia and euphoric energy.

Shall I say grace, give thanks
for being a broom, brush, handle?
recognition eludes me; an ephemeral existence
a transitory toy; a yellow submarine (we all live in one)
a Fisher-Price label, pleasurable plastic . . .

I just want to be myself,
discard this mediocre mask of unreality

But . . . what is the real thing in life's incessant stream?
Will my restless test be rewarded
in the recycling bin?

And what is the *real* thing? Pepsi? or Coke?

Judy Studd

Rainsteps

In the grey and misted morning
A steady falling of rainsteps
Creating pathways and journeys
Reminders of some deep and unlit sea
A widening web of possibility
Evolving to destiny
Refreshing parched desert and dry stone
Sweeping the land in silver tresses
Gentle kisses against sleeping skin
Now the rainsteps fall
Flowers heavy with light
Wings unfolded and feather soft
Glimpses of paradise and sadness
Towers and spires against the horizon
In the restless clouds
Visitors from the other world
Tender is the call
Yet silently powerful
Breaking against the highest wall

Paul Andrew Jones

Just A Message

It's right, it's wrong, it's out, it's in,
It's good or bad, it's clean or sin,
We each have views, on what's to be,
But someone else's view, we don't always see.
We all know basically, what's kind and good,
But do we behave, like we should,
Heal all bad tidings, prevent suffering,
Evils slip away, but love will cling.

Look at ourselves, investigate,
There's so much love, and so much hate,
We know it's there, but we don't like seeing,
That it's in each average, human being.
It can't be right, to be this way,
So let's be more loving, every day,
Because living and loving, is all I want to do,
And this is just a message, I send to you.

Jeff Hobson

Betrayed

I see the hatred in your eyes,
As I, your mother, you now despise.
Time and again your tricks display,
For others to think my minds' astray.
At ninety-two, at times confused,
Your little games leave me bemused.
My money I kept hid away,
When my back was turned, it seemed to stray.
You'd scream and shout to wear me down,
Then hit me, make me cry and frown.
My pensions to place in your name,
Now I know your little game.
Into your bank each weekly amount,
To pay for your holidays, in your account?
Behind my back your plan did seek,
'Stay in the home for just a week?'
If by then for my home I yearn,
To my little bungalow I can return?
My home was all gone my mid-week,
My belongings gone, I feel so bleak.
Made yourselves keeper of my purse,
Stopped my money, you I did curse.
Against your older sister, behind her back,
Selfish actions, as love you lack.
The years are long in the day,
My life soon will slip away.
You've made me ill, though all I've done,
You'll not feel guilty, your battles won.

Josie Minton

110

My Daughter

From the moment you were born
All of my dreams came true
As all I ever wanted
Was a little girl like you

How the years together have flown
And you my darling grown
No longer a baby small
But a child of beauty known

With your long hair to your waist
And your beautiful face
You are my pride and joy
You are my world, my life, my own

I've taught you manners and to be polite
You've taught me 'How to get it right'
'Yes' there have been times
When I can be quite stern
And I raise my voice to you
Only to let you 'learn'
But we have so much love to give
That the sterner times are few

I hope that you will grow up caring and giving
For you my child are the reasons for me living
As I know there have been times
When I have felt at an all time low
But then I look at you and I know
How lucky I am to have a daughter like you
You are my world, my life, my own.

J L Jackson

Conundrum

What breaks but does not ever fall?
Or falls but does not break?
Our days and nights, we know, are all
alike to those who take
no trouble to examine life
and take the time to sit
and ponder, without mental strife,
just why our sun was lit
so that each new day will break
yet will not fall and smash
and night, in which our dreams we make,
falls without a crash.

   D G W Garde

Pisces Rising

Eyes of the fortune-teller swimming
like piranhas in a cornflakes bowl;
Slowly, scarlet curtain rising
on family life;
Pain, strife, love where we can,
all down to God for a poor show
put on by breakfast soldiers
frowning at the clock;
Baby's crying, your turn
(some of us have a living to earn,
not to mention a train to miss);
What, no kiss? A dog's life this,
I'll say! And the devil to pay
for clothes, car, phone;
Alone, or so it seems.

Whatever happened,
to dreams?

R N Taber

Cromwell

As a land owner he was on the right track,
But as a soldier he never looked back.
But, first at school he did very well,
He was known as Oliver Cromwell.
As far as we know he had good health,
His family had land and wealth.
But local administration he had a part to play,
And with the parliamentary army he did stay.
Commanding his own cavalry regiment,
Against the royalist he was sent.
Nothing this roundhead could not tackle,
Successful in all sieges and battle.
His army played a major role in parliamentary victory,
The battle was sealed in June 1645 he won at Naseby.
Civil war flared up again and the royalist fled,
After his trail the royalist king lost his head.
Cromwell attributed his success to God's will,
Historians pointed to this courage and skill.
His care in training and equipping his men,
And his tight discipline over the fen.
He became Lord Protector, an important key,
He brought peace in the troubled period of British history.

Margaret Upson

Happy Birthday Granddaughter Samantha

In the picture you are like a film star,
We love you even being so afar,
Samantha's eyes say grandparents are best,
Who always know that Samantha is blessed.

Grandchildren are to us wondrous gifts,
They gave grandparents wondrous uplifts,
Your smile and looks that gave us brighter life,
Spend Golden Day of April in your stride.

May God guide you always through each life's storm;
Rewards come from Heaven when it's cold or warm,
Do always have faith in yourself and God,
Do remember footsteps parents trod.

Then you will grow into beautiful star,
We love you however you are afar,
We think you have blaze of a star beauty,
Study figures of speech as a duty.

School teacher will make you richer each day,
Make literature story of the day;
Forgive me inflict all this on you,
Meanwhile, I must bring all this subjects on too.

Let us say you must not walk on your own,
Mem say until much older you have grown,
Children must open their eyes before they leap,
Books are precious, we ought them to keep.

Milan Trubarac

It Takes A Brave Lady

Cars were slowing down
There lay a man on the ground
People stared
No one stopped or dared to care

Accept a lady of Irish descent
With me over the man bent
Begging touch him to 'see he's alright"
(Just the thought filled me with fright!)

With glasses ledged on end of nose
I studied him from head to toes
Then seeing movement of his chest
Convinced me I had done my best

I diagnosed he was asleep
Or maybe in a coma deep
softly in her accent charming
She asked 'are you ok me darlin?'

Awakening he looked aghast
'Aye' he hicc'd 'I'm glad you asked'
Back he went to rest his head
The sun his light the grass his bed

Just suppose it had been worse
I'm no hero I'm no nurse
School rules should enforce
That we take a first aid course

Pam Brown

March Wind

Once again the wind is blowing
Now that March season is showing.
It blows and whistles all around
Making such an eerie sound.
Seeming to say 'I'm here to stay',
Blowing all your cares away
Sometimes warm, sometimes cold,
As it rustles through the trees
And blows at the leaves.
Through your hair and all around
Oh what a fantastic sound!
No one knows where it comes from
Or why it is so
But when it arrives we really do know.

Joan Erskine

Insecurities

Please tell me, when you look at me,
What is it exactly that you see?
Could it be ugliness - is that so?
Is it my make-up - do I need more?
What's on your mind when you look with that frown?
Do you think I'm attractive or maybe a 'clown'?
Should I lose weight - do you think I'm fat?
Are my ears too big - should I wear a hat?
Would you say I'm quiet - or possibly shy?
Maybe I don't shut up and you're wondering why?
Are my teeth stained - is my breath bad?
Do I have BO - do you think I'm really 'sad'?
Are there occasions when I look good?
Should I make a bit more effort? If only I could!

I wish this face and body wasn't the image 'I' saw,
To be pretty and to like myself is all I ask for.
You see, I know I have dilemmas and I fret a lot,
I try hard to ignore them but insecurities I've got!

Keri Garvey

Soldiers

As the bombs whiz over and past my head
We lay cowering with guns filled with deadly lead;
Our shelter was hit today - it just crumbled
The bombs are falling and many are stumbled.
Our leader is leaving us and going into the city,
Every day we see people fleeing, we all feel pity.
As we walk along what once was the main roads
We see people lying dead while others carry loads.
One day I'm handing out food and the next I'm killing,
We see soldiers and others, blood spilling.
Each of us hoping and wishing for something better
Today from my wife came a letter.
I think of what my wife and I had, then my heart is suddenly sore
What did I have before this silly war?
Most importantly a family, I also had a job and house,
Now all I have for company is a friendly mouse.
I hope that I will be with my family soon,
But I think they have the boon.

Naomi Wynn (13)

Kosovo

Another day, another tear,
with people full of fear.
Husbands lost
with a killing frost.
Wailing mothers and children loaded on and off trucks
Who loves them; who cares?
They have no home
not a phone;
lives are wrecked.
Torn from home; torn from hope, from life.
They have lost everything
some even their lives.
They have crossed the border in their thousands
all is well; all is safe for now
but will it last?

Ben Wynn (10)

A Home By The Sea

I would like a home in sight of the sea
Just to breathe in the salty air
And know that where new buildings may be
They just can't build them there

No walls or fences in front of me
No traffic or town noises for me
Maybe a boat ot two sailing by
And the everlasting call of the sea

To see the colour changes of the ocean
From blue to grey to green
To see the space that meets the horizon
I see it all in my dreams

Watch waters enter and fill the caves
It bubbles splashes then swirls back to the sea
If the sea had a voice I think it would say
Who is there anywhere who can stop me

Its calm and warm and gentle
When beneath the sunshine heat
And the ebb tide as it flows to and fro
Shifts the sand beneath your feet

But the ever-changing face of the sea
Can be angry pounding cliffs of the shoreline
And little boats cling to the harbour side
When wayward winds and wild waters combine

Adela Llewellyn

First Light

Postie we all like on the pavement riding a bike
Taxi cabs racing across the town unable to slow down.
Life in a matchbox everyone playing catch fox
Far over morning the day is dawning.

V Scytere

A Blade Of Grass

Simplicity itself,
Or so it may seem,
But who lives on Earth,
That can make it exist?

Chemistry can say,
What composes it,
Biology tells that,
It depends on light.

It grows from a seed,
And depends on soil,
Rain pours on it,
And up it exists.

But as clever as we are,
How stupid we seem,
For no-one on Earth,
Can make the ground green.

We can drop seeds,
And up grass can grow,
All over the world,
In each country sow.

But nobody lives now,
Who can make a seed from scratch.
As easy as that!
But what do we lack?

The know how,
That's what!
'Cos the secret of creation,
May exist in vegetation.

David Sawyer

Leave Your Cards On The Table

There he would go on the rampage of sin
Deck of cards in his pocket
Thinking of the poker game he was hoping to win.
His mother a widow oft' times said to him
Lay your cards on the table tonight son,
Lay your cards on the table tonight.

He went on unheeding his sinful way,
All night at the card table oft' he did stay.
Returning one morning there he found
His poor widow mother dying alone.
A soft whisper was all she could say,
Put the cards on the table today son,
Put the cards on the table today.

How his heart ached how he did cry,
Amidst his sobs he whispered goodbye.
Mam the cards on the table
That brought a weak smile,
With the cards on the table son,
I'm happy to die.

Frances Gibson

A Friend In Deed

A friend in deed is a friend indeed.

A step back, or a word back, no friend in deed;
but echoes of darkness that precedes.

A friend, a weed that lacked the deed
that flowered of their own selfish need.

A friend is a provider and sower of seed.

You are my flower because of need.
You are my friend because of deed.

My love for you does not lack the hope.
You are my seed.

Timothy John Cook

Despair

Desolation settles around me like a cloud
Despair that would do the cursed proud
Loneliness wraps me in its shroud
Alone alone in the mingling crowd.

Empty eyes with vacant stares
Haunt my dreams and stop my prayers
Alone I am an island in the sea
My companion living death from which I cannot flee.

Tis a cruel world that takes all you give
You question your existence, the reason to live
Is it all damned to despair?
Why should I even care?

Is love such that it takes all you give?
Rips you apart into pieces you'd sieve
Permeates your senses, causes such pain
Feelings enough to drive you insane.

'To have loved and lost' is better they say
In my living hell I don't believe it's this way
What is there left for me to do?
To leave you, damn you and condemn me too.

Time heals all so the learned say
But life is short and I want to live every day
The pain I feel is too real to go away
Cannot be healed in any way . . .

Seema Khehar

Lost Love

When the heart is near to breaking,
battle on your lonely road.
When grief and pain seem like a mountain,
time will heal: a lighter load.

Until that day when time has passed,
when moonlight lights your way.
Better far to pray forgiveness,
paint a picture that will stay.

Be brave and strong when nights are long,
though yearning break of day.
Give thanks for all you have been given,
enjoy the memories on display.

Many questions may be painful,
cruel is this woeful world.
Remember all the joyous moments,
happiness will then unfurl.

Nature's gifts dispensed so freely,
help us through our troubled days.
Almighty hands that guide us gently,
treading paths trod many ways.

Silence weaves its lonely web,
around a heart that's broken.
Keep striving onwards and believe,
the thoughts not always spoken.

Alwyn James

The Scene

(Dedicated to my niece Lisa)

Warehouse, jumping
to the incessant beat.
Dancers grooving
in the steamy heat.
Jungle, house, garage
music, what a treat.
Popping E's
and guzzling water
oh so sweet.
Sweating bodies
writhing closer
someone new to meet?
What a buzz
this scene
just so complete.
Pure energy
the high of highs
look at the dancers eyes
as bright as rainbows
in the dark skies.
The beat goes on and on
like tribal drums of old
the young love it
on this idea, they're well and truly sold.

Ian Mowatt

The Love Of God

So many years ago our Lord looked down and smiled
He saw how much we needed
Him and then gave us a gift
The gift of love was always ours
We just did not know
Some sign was needed to show how much
And so to us He gave His Son
To prove His love for all to see.

On that cold night the star did show
The way to love
The way to God
In a lonely barn that night long ago
Our Lord was born so gentle so small
But the love therein so great to all

Who dared to look
Who dared to find
The love of God here on the Earth

That love was there
That love is here
For all who choose to listen to His word
As spoken to the Children of God
As spoken to the followers of Christ

Love to hold
Love to share
Love for all on Christmas day
Love all the days of our lives
The love of God for all His children

Fiona Higgins

Enigma

The light was there a burning flame
like moths we gathered in her train
she had a gift only Gods bestow.
How fortunate were we before she had to go
to receive the gifts she did bestow.
The gifts she gave are hard to tell
to each she gave relief from Hell.

John E Lindsay

Tales Of Spices Poem

Spikenard, Calmus, Saffron, Cinnamon,
Come into my orchards
And taste the fruits divine
Let the aroma of Spikenard
Calmus, Saffron, Cinnamon
Be for ever Thine.

Based on Solomon's Song Chapter 4 Verse 13-16

Stacte, Onycha, Galbanum
Moses was told by the Lord
To make a perfume
And it was to be sweet spices
Stacte, Onycha, Galbanum
And with pure Frankincense
Was laid in the Tabernacle
And the spices were most holy
For the Lord.

Based on Exodus Chapter 30 Verse 34

Mustard
Plant the seed in the field
Watch how big it grows
Turning into a Mustard tree
For birds to go to and fro
In days to come
It will be a spice and a home

Based on Matthew Chapter 13 Verse 31

Coriander
Moses and the Israelites
Sowed the seeds to make Manna
It was to be like Coriander seed
White, flaky and it filled peoples need.

Based on Exodus Chapter 16 Verse 31

Denise Thomson